THE GREAT™
AMERICAN
HISTORY
QUIZ

# Heroes and Villains

# Heroes and Villains

Series Created by
**Abbe Raven and Dana Calderwood**

Written by
**Charles Nordlander, Howard Blumenthal, Dana Calderwood and Robert Sharenow** with additional questions by **John Aherne**

WARNER BOOKS

A Time Warner Company

If you purchased this book without a cover you should be aware that this book may have been stolen property and reported as "unsold and destroyed" to the publisher. In such case neither the author nor the publisher has received any payment for this "stripped book."

Copyright ©2001 by A&E Television.
The History Channel, the "H" logo, and the Great American History Quiz are trademarks of A&E Television and are registered in the United States and other countries. All rights reserved.

Warner Books, Inc., 1271 Avenue of the Americas,
New York, NY 10020

Visit our Web site at www.twbookmark.com

For information on Time Warner Trade Publishing's
online publishing program, visit www.ipublish.com

 A Time Warner Company

Printed in the United States of America

First Printing: June 2001
10 9 8 7 6 5 4 3 2 1

Library of Congress Cataloging-in-Publication Data

    The great American history quiz : heroes and villains / the History Channel.
      p. cm.
    ISBN 0-446-67687-X
    1. United States—Biography—Miscellanea.  2. United States—History—Miscellanea.  3. Celebrities—United States—Biography—Miscellanea.  I. History Channel (Television network).

    CT215.G74  2001
    920.73—dc21                                  2001017926

Cover design by Carolyn Lechter
Cover photographs by Corbis/Time Pix
Book design and text composition by Ralph Fowler

---

### ATTENTION: SCHOOLS AND CORPORATIONS

WARNER books are available at quantity discounts with bulk purchase for educational, business, or sales promotional use. For information, please write to: SPECIAL SALES DEPARTMENT, WARNER BOOKS, 1271 AVENUE OF THE AMERICAS, NEW YORK, N.Y. 10020

**America has had its share of the good, the bad, and the downright ugly. That's why we've devoted this edition of <u>The Great American History Quiz</u> to the famous heroes and villains of American history.**

**1.** "I have not yet begun to fight!" Those chilling words were spoken by John Paul Jones, America's first great naval hero. Jones led his ship, the *Bonhomme Richard*, to a thrilling victory against a fifty-gun British vessel, the *Serapis*. In the heat of battle the two ships became hooked together—but they continued the fight, hull to hull, until finally the British surrendered. The question is: Which war was Jones fighting at the time?

**(a)** The Revolutionary War

**(b)** The French and Indian War

**(c)** The War of 1812

HEROES AND VILLAINS

★ 1 ★

**ANSWER**

The answer is **(a)**. Jones won the battle but lost his ship: The *Bonhomme Richard* sank from damage after the British surrendered. Later, as you know, John Paul Jones launched his remarkable second career as Led Zeppelin's bass player. We're kidding, of course.

Actor Gary Cooper portrayed World War I hero Sergeant Alvin York in a very popular movie named for the soldier. York himself was an outstanding marksman who won the Congressional Medal of Honor. He had boldly taken on a German machine-gun nest and single-handedly killed twenty-five German soldiers—then 132 more surrendered to York and the seven men he was leading. But in truth, York had been deeply reluctant to join the war effort. What was the reason?

**(a)** He was losing his eyesight

**(b)** He was deeply religious

**(c)** His parents were German immigrants

**(d)** He was notoriously afraid of flying

**ANSWER**

The answer is **(b)**. Although deeply religious, York was denied status as a conscientious objector and was drafted. Sergeant Alvin York was truly a reluctant hero.

**3** General George S. Patton Jr. was a brilliant military strategist whose command of tank warfare proved decisive in World War II. "Old Blood and Guts" captured Palermo in 1943. He followed that success by leading troops across Europe, resulting in the capture of 100,000 German troops in 1945. Patton led by example: He was the model of discipline and bravery. But sometimes Patton went too far. What 1943 incident brought him unwanted headlines?

**(a)** He criticized FDR's leadership

**(b)** His troops tortured a German prisoner

**(c)** His tanks purposely demolished several German museums and churches

**(d)** He slapped a hospitalized soldier

**ANSWER**

The answer is **(d)**. Patton slapped a crying, battle-fatigued soldier in the hospital and called him a coward. This was Patton's second such "slapping" incident, and he was told to apologize. Patton did no such thing. The unrepentant general considered the hospital tent full of wounded soldiers a place of honor and that this particular soldier who was not physically wounded had no place being there. Sometimes even heroes make errors in judgment.

**4** But General Patton wasn't just a war hero—he was an Olympic hero as well. Patton represented the United States in the 1912 Olympics at Stockholm in the modern pentathlon: an event consisting of shooting, fencing, swimming, riding, and running. How did Patton fare in the Olympics?

**(a)** He was disqualified

**(b)** Fifth place

**(c)** Bronze medal

**(d)** Gold medal

**ANSWER**

**(b).** General Patton placed a very respectable fifth place in the modern pentathlon.

 Patton was an Olympic champion, a brave soldier, and one of the military's greatest commanders. Not a bad résumé. But how did this great American hero die?

**(a)** Killed while on a safari in Africa

**(b)** Killed in battle during WW II

**(c)** Drowned while sailing a boat to Hawaii

**(d)** Died as a result of injuries sustained in a car accident

**ANSWER**

**(d)**. For a man who put himself in danger throughout his entire life, General Patton died a surprisingly pedestrian death. He died a few days after an automobile he was riding in was hit by a truck. He is buried in Luxembourg.

 While we're on the topic of war, who can forget being glued to their television sets during Operation Desert Storm—we couldn't tear our eyes away from Saddam Hussein, SCUD missiles, Patriot missiles, and Wolf Blitzer. And we cheered when the ceasefire took effect on April 17, 1991. Who was the man in command of Operation Desert Storm?

**(a)** Colin Powell

**(b)** Calvin Waller

**(c)** Norman Schwarzkopf

**(d)** Peter Dobbins

**ANSWER**

**(c).** Stormin' Norman Schwarzkopf was the commander in chief of Operation Desert Storm.

THE GREAT AMERICAN HISTORY QUIZ

 We all admire people who can get great bargains: the people who wind up buying million-dollar paintings at garage sales or the kid who buys the baseball card for fifty cents that eventually sells for $10,000. But perhaps one of the best deals in history was when one of the early American settlers bought the island of Manhattan from the Native Americans for approximately twenty-four dollars. Who was this heroic bargain hunter?

**(a)** Sir George Carteret

**(b)** Peter Minuit

**(c)** Peter Stuyvesant

**(d)** Piet Hein

**ANSWER**

**(b).** Talk about a blue light special. For sixty Dutch guilders, which was roughly twenty-four dollars, Peter Minuit bought the island of Manhattan. If he had that twenty-four dollars today, Peter Minuit might be able to afford a movie with a large popcorn.

**America has always had a bizarre love affair with gangsters—those fedora-wearing, gun-toting men who kill first and ask questions later. Here are a few questions about America's most notorious gangsters.**

**8** Al Capone started his crime career as a knife-scarred kid in Brooklyn. But he hit the big time in Chicago, where he ruthlessly ruled an army of as many as a thousand mobsters. They worked for Capone's illicit empire built up of booze, brothels, gambling, and restaurants. By 1927 he had amassed a fortune worth one hundred million dollars. The question is: How old was Al Capone when he took over as Chicago's top crime boss?

**(a)** 25

**(b)** 40

**(c)** 55

**(d)** 75

**ANSWER**

The answer is **(a)**. Capone and his boss, Johnny Torrio, took over the Chicago rackets from Big Jim Colosimo the easy way—they had him rubbed out. Then, after Torrio retired, Capone was left alone at the top.

 Al Capone's most notorious mob hit occurred in 1929, when his henchmen killed six members of bootlegger George "Bugs" Moran's North Side gang (a seventh victim wasn't one of Bugs's men—he was just in the wrong place at the wrong time). Although Capone was in Florida at the time of the killing, his men did quite a number, pumping 150 bullets into the bodies of the seven victims. On what day did this massacre occur?

**(a)** New Year's Day

**(b)** St. Valentine's Day

**(c)** St. Patrick's Day

**(d)** Christmas Day

**ANSWER**

**(b).** This brutal killing took place on February 14 and has since been known as the St. Valentine's Day Massacre.

**10** The feds had been trying to get their hands on Capone for years, but a strict code of silence kept him out of reach of the law. But as the saying goes, no good (or bad) deed goes unpunished. For what crime was Al Capone eventually incarcerated?

**(a)** Murder

**(b)** Counterfeiting

**(c)** Grand larceny

**(d)** Tax evasion

**HEROES AND VILLAINS**

### ANSWER

**(d).** You can fool all of the people some of the time and some of the people all of the time, but you can't fool the IRS. Although he had once served a brief sentence for weapons possession and was held overnight in jail after being arrested for murder, it wasn't until 1931 that the law was able to put Capone away for tax evasion.

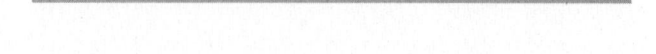

**11** At the end of the Roaring Twenties, a street kid named Lucky Luciano took over New York City's crime empire. Lucky got his nickname by winning at craps and dodging the cops. But he never left "business" to chance. By controlling the prostitution, gambling, and drug rackets, Luciano lived in luxury at a time when other Americans were selling apples on street corners. Luciano was considered lucky for another reason too. What did he do?

**(a)** Acquire the patent for nylon

**(b)** Sell his life story for $1 million

**(c)** Live for more than 60 years

**(d)** Win one of the first national lotteries

**A N S W E R**

The answer is **(c)**. In fact, he luckily survived one of those notorious "one-way rides" for gangsters: Henchmen stabbed him with an ice pick, slit his throat, then left him for dead. But Lucky lived. Decades later, while meeting a producer, Luciano suddenly clutched his heart and died. They were about to make a deal for his life story. But his luck had run out.

**12** John Dillinger was one of the most famous bank robbers in American history, a gunman with a dapper sense of style long before John Gotti made the headlines. By all accounts, Dillinger had a sharp eye for cash, flashy clothes, and the ladies. And it was a woman—the famous "woman in red"—who led police to Chicago's Biograph Theater, where they gunned down Dillinger. The question is: How long did Dillinger's career in bank robbery last?

**(a)** Seven months

**(b)** One year

**(c)** Six years

**(d)** Twelve years

**ANSWER**

The answer is **(b)** one year. For all his notoriety, Dillinger didn't rob banks for very long. He started in June of 1933 and was shot dead the following summer.

**13** Bonnie and Clyde are perhaps two of America's most famous villains. Notorious for their robberies, their murders, and their knack for avoiding the law at every turn, their escapades made front-page headlines all across the country, and their lives are now the stuff of legend. How long did Bonnie and Clyde's crime spree last?

**(a)** Two years

**(b)** Five years

**(c)** Ten years

**(d)** Fifteen years

### 13

**ANSWER**

**(a).** Like John Dillinger's, Bonnie and Clyde's life of crime was relatively short. Although Clyde and his brother had been lawbreakers for virtually their entire lives, Clyde didn't meet Bonnie until 1929—and he was incarcerated soon afterward. It was only after his parole in 1932 that he and Bonnie started their cross-country capers, which ended in 1934.

 And how did Bonnie and Clyde's life on the lam end?

**(a)** No one really knows

**(b)** Clyde was killed, Bonnie was sentenced to life in prison

**(c)** Bonnie was killed, Clyde was sentenced to life in prison

**(d)** They were both killed

## 14

**ANSWER**

**(d)**. They fought the law, and the law won. After nearly two years of murder, thievery, kidnapping, and bank heists, Bonnie and Clyde were killed in a police ambush on May 23, 1934. Ironically, the man who issued the order to open fire was a frequent patron in the restaurant in which Bonnie used to work as a waitress.

 And one last question about these American icons. True or false: Bonnie and Clyde were husband and wife.

**ANSWER**

**False**. Bonnie and Clyde never married each other. Actually, Bonnie was technically a married woman when she took up with Clyde. When she was sixteen she married a man named Roy Thorton, who was arrested for burglary soon after their wedding. Clearly, Bonnie had a thing for bad boys.

**You know, history is filled with "real-life" good guys like Patton and bad guys like Bonnie and Clyde. But for decades, some of our most memorable heroes and villains have been slugging it out in the comics. How much do you remember about them? We'll name the comic supervillain, you name the hero.**

**16** The bad guy was the self-proclaimed emperor of the universe, Planet Mongo's Ming the Merciless. Who was the man who set the good citizens of Mongo free?

**ANSWER**

Under the leadership of the brave Earthman **Flash Gordon**, the people of Mongo won their freedom.

**17** Prune Face, the Mole, and Flattop performed evil deeds in a Chet Gould comic strip. Who was the good guy who stopped them?

## 17

**ANSWER**

**Dick Tracy** is one of America's longest-running heroes. He nabbed his first bad guys in 1931 and he hasn't stopped yet.

**18** If you read DC comic books in the 1960s, you knew the mischievous imp from the fifth dimension Mr. Mxyzptlk. Name the superhero whom Mr. Mxyzptlk harassed.

### 18

**ANSWER**

**Superman** discovered various ways to send Mr. Mxyzptlk back where he came from. Our favorite was to trick the little guy into saying his name backward.

**Nothing says "villain" like breaking the sixth commandment: "Thou shalt not kill." Let's ask some questions about people who are famous for having done just that.**

## 19

Around the time of her famous trial, this morbid little rhyme became popular:

*Lizzie Borden took an ax*
*And gave her mother 40 whacks*
*And when she saw what she had done*
*She gave her father 41.*

But although the public was largely convinced that she had done the bloody deed, Lizzie Borden was never found guilty of murdering her father and stepmother. On what grounds was she acquitted?

**(a)** She acted in self-defense

**(b)** There was insufficient evidence

**(c)** She was declared insane

**(d)** Because of a police procedural error

## 19

**ANSWER**

The answer is **(b)**. Lizzie Borden spoke only two sentences at her trial: "I am innocent" and "I leave it to my counsel to speak for me." That was enough, and the circumstantial evidence wasn't sufficient to convict her. But strong suspicions of guilt followed Lizzie Borden to her grave. By the way: The same house in Fall River, Massachusetts, in which the ax murders took place is now an inn, called the Lizzie Borden Bed and Breakfast Museum.

**20** Nathan Leopold and Richard Loeb had everything going for them, including youth, brains, and lots of money. But in 1924 they kidnapped and killed fourteen-year-old Bobby Franks just for the "intellectual" thrill of committing the perfect murder. Unexpectedly, the body was discovered, along with Leopold's eyeglasses. Finally, Leopold and Loeb confessed, then faced sentencing. Which brilliant defense attorney convinced a judge not to execute them?

**(a)** Clarence Darrow

**(b)** Earl Warren

**(c)** Thurgood Marshall

**(d)** Robert Crowe

## 20

**ANSWER**

The answer is **(a)** Clarence Darrow. The judge sentenced Leopold and Loeb to life plus ninety-nine years. Loeb was later killed in prison, but Leopold—despite the long sentence—was released on parole in 1958 and died in 1971.

**21** Clarence Darrow's closing argument in the Leopold and Loeb trial, during which he convinced Judge John R. Caverly to spare their lives, is considered to be one of the finest moments of Darrow's career and one of the most convincing closing arguments on legal record. After the Leopold and Loeb case, Clarence Darrow went on to appear as defense counsel in an even more celebrated case. Which case was it?

**(a)** Sacco and Vanzetti

**(b)** The Scopes monkey trial

**(c)** Mills Hall

**(d)** The Scottsboro 9

**HEROES AND VILLAINS**

## 21

### ANSWER

**(b)**. Clarence Darrow defended John Thomas Scopes (more on him later). Darrow eventually lost the case to William Jennings Bryan, but interest in the trial was so high that it was the first trial in American history to be broadcast live over the radio.

**22** On January 15, 1947, the body of a young woman was found in a vacant lot in the Leimert Park section of Los Angeles. The body of Elizabeth Short had been cut completely in half at the abdomen, and its discovery launched one of the most famous murder cases in U.S. history. Although the villain who perpetrated this crime was never captured, the nickname given to the brutally murdered up-and-coming starlet dominated the news for over a year. By what nickname was Elizabeth Short known?

**(a)** Terry Torso

**(b)** Bad Luck Betty

**(c)** The Black Widow

**(d)** The Black Dahlia

### ANSWER

**(d)**. During her life, Elizabeth Short was given the name Black Dahlia because of her inky black hair and her penchant for wearing black clothes. Her murder was declared "unsolved" because the prime suspect was killed while smoking a cigarette in bed.

**23** On January 17, 1977, a young man waited silently, a hood over his head and a target over his heart. Then a Utah firing squad ended a four-year ban on capital punishment in America. The executed murderer was Gary Gilmore, who made national headlines by refusing to appeal his own death sentence. In fact, Gilmore's case attracted the attention of author Norman Mailer, who wrote a Pulitzer prize-winning novel about the lifelong criminal. What was the title of Mailer's book?

**(a)** *In Cold Blood*

**(b)** *The Executioner's Song*

**(c)** *Shot in the Heart*

**(d)** *Dead Man Walking*

## 23

**ANSWER**

The answer is **(b)** *The Executioner's Song*. But the other choices were close: Truman Capote's *In Cold Blood* is based on a real murder case, *Shot in the Heart* is the family memoir by Gilmore's brother Mikal, and *Dead Man Walking* is the story of death-row inmate Patrick Sonnier.

**24** When Harvey Milk was elected to the San Francisco Board of Supervisors in 1977, he became the first openly gay man in the history of the United States to win any substantial political office. He and San Francisco's mayor, George Mascone, were assassinated on November 27, 1978, by conservative, antigay, former board member Dan White, who confessed to, and was convicted of, the murders. What sentence did Dan White receive for this double murder?

**(a)** Five years with parole

**(b)** One hundred years

**(c)** Life without parole

**(d)** The death sentence

## 24

**ANSWER**

**(a).** After a psychologist testified that the amount of junk food Dan White consumed probably led to a deep depression (the infamous "Twinkie defense"), the jury sympathized with the murderer and gave him just five years in prison with parole—a sentence that sparked many protests and riots on the streets of San Francisco.

**25** In one of the most tragic events in American history, 914 people (276 of which were children) committed mass suicide—most of them by drinking Kool-Aid mixed with cyanide—during the Jonestown massacre of November 18, 1978. Once a popular pastor, and founder of the thriving People's Temple, the Reverend Jim Jones ordered his followers to kill themselves when he feared he would be arrested for the murder of U.S. Representative Leo Ryan. In what country did the Jonestown massacre take place?

**(a)** The United States

**(b)** Brazil

**(c)** Uruguay

**(d)** Guyana

## 25

### ANSWER

**(d).** The South American country of Guyana was the site of the Jonestown massacre.

THE GREAT AMERICAN HISTORY QUIZ

**Heroes not only save lives, they enrich our lives with their arms, legs, and feats—of athletic prowess. For America, many of our nation's proudest moments have occurred at the Olympics.**

### 26

In 1936, on the world stage of the Berlin Olympic Games, Jesse Owens became a national hero. He won four gold medals, shattering Hitler's myth of Aryan supremacy. After returning to the United States, Owens recalled, "I wasn't invited to shake hands with Hitler, but I wasn't invited to the White House to shake hands with the president either." Jesse's Olympic gold never led to the riches that sports heroes enjoy today. Which of the following did Owens sometimes do to earn money after the Olympics?

**(a)** Act in B-movies

**(b)** Endorse sneakers in radio commercials

**(c)** Run races against horses and dogs

**(d)** Perform in circuses

HEROES AND VILLAINS

## 26

### ANSWER

The answer is **(c)**. "People said it was degrading for an Olympic champion to run against a horse," said Owens, "but what was I supposed to do? I had four gold medals, but you can't eat four gold medals." In 1976 Owens received the Presidential Medal of Freedom from President Ford. It is America's highest civilian honor, and one that Jesse Owens long deserved.

**27** Cassius Clay was a brash eighteen-year-old who rose to fame at the 1960 Summer Olympics in Rome. He won a gold medal in boxing and proudly wore it for days afterward. But for some, Clay the hero became Muhammad Ali the villain when he refused to fight in Vietnam for religious reasons. Ali was found guilty of violating the draft laws, then stripped of his world heavyweight title and banned from boxing. In time, the Supreme Court would overturn his conviction, and Ali returned to the ring. The question is, who'd he knock out to win back his title?

**(a)** George Foreman

**(b)** Joe Frazier

**(c)** Leon Spinks

**(d)** Sonny Liston

## 27

**ANSWER**

The answer is **(a)**. George Foreman. In 1996 Muhammad Ali was selected to light the torch to start the Summer Games in Atlanta. He was once again an Olympic hero.

**28** You might say that Babe Didrikson Zaharias had a knack for sports. She rocked in baseball, softball, football, swimming, figure skating—even billiards and marbles! But those weren't her best sports. Zaharias was also an All-American basketball player and track star who rose to fame during the 1932 Olympics. She won gold medals in two of the following three sports—in which sport did Babe NOT take home the gold?

**(a)** Hurdles

**(b)** Javelin

**(c)** Golf

## 28

**ANSWER**

The answer is **(c)**. Golf is not an Olympic sport, but Zaharias did take up the game for fun. Fun?! She won seventeen straight tournaments in 1947—not even Tiger Woods has matched that record. Zaharias went on to win the U.S. Women's Open in 1950 and then, in the midst of battling cancer, she did it again in 1954.

**29** One of the most riveting moments at the 1996 Olympics in Atlanta was the women's gymnastics competition. The American team was in the lead and on its way to winning America's first-ever gold medal in the team competition. All that was needed was a solid score on the vault. The only problem was that the last girl in the rotation had already torn a ligament in her ankle and could barely feel her leg. Undaunted, she took her place on the runway, leaped onto the springboard . . . and while the rest of the world bit their nails, this gutsy athlete nailed the landing (tearing a second ligament in the process), guaranteeing the United States a gold medal. Who made this world-famous landing?

**(a)** Shannon Miller

**(b)** Dominique Dawes

**(c)** Dominique Moceanu

**(d)** Kerri Strug

## 29

**ANSWER**

**(d)**. Kerri Strug became a national hero for her successful vault.

**30** Another American became a hero by, well, *not* winning the Olympic Games. Dan Jansen, the world-record holder in speedskating for the 500 and 1,000 meters, seemed cursed at the Olympic Games. In the 1988 Games in Calgary he fell in both the 500- and the 1,000-meter speedskating races—races that took place almost immediately after Dan's beloved sister died. And in Albertville in 1992, Dan Jansen slipped twice in both races and came home empty-handed. Did Dan Jansen ever win an Olympic medal?

### 30

**ANSWER**

**Yes.** Sometimes stories do have happy endings. After a run of spectacularly bad luck, Dan Jansen finally took Olympic gold in the 1,000 meters at the 1994 Games in Lillehammer.

**31** Unfortunately, the Olympics has had its share of villains as well. At the Munich Games in 1972, eight Arab commandos broke into the Olympic compound in West Germany. They shot and killed two Israelis outright, one a wrestling coach, the other a weightlifting coach. The commandos then took nine others of the eighteen-member Israeli Olympic team hostage and settled into the compound for a siege. After much negotiation, the hostage situation quickly turned into a massacre. The question: How many Israeli athletes were killed?

**(a)** 2

**(b)** 4

**(c)** 9

**(d)** 11

**HEROES AND VILLAINS**

**ANSWER**

**(d)**. In one of the worst tragedies of the Olympic Games, eleven members of the Israeli Olympic team were killed in Munich in 1972.

**Serial killers: They grab headlines, strike fear in our hearts, and years after their crimes are committed, we can't help thinking about them when the lights are out and we hear a strange noise outside. Serial killers are perhaps the most terrifying villains of all. So turn on the lights, make sure the door is locked, and try to answer the next five questions about serial killers and their victims.**

**32** One of the most terrifying serial killers in recent years was David Berkowitz, aka the Son of Sam. He began his killing spree on July 29, 1976, when he murdered Donna Lauria and injured her friend Jody Valenti in the Bronx, New York. Six murders and seven attempted murders later, the Son of Sam was finally arrested. How did David Berkowitz come up with his nickname?

**(a)** His father's name was Sam

**(b)** He had a childhood dog named Sam

**(c)** His neighbor's name was Sam

**(d)** From the Bible

## 32

**ANSWER**

**(c)**. In David Berkowitz's delusional world, his neighbor Sam Carr was the host of a powerful demon named Sam who was in the employ of General Jack Cosmo, supreme ruler of the devil dogs running throughout New York City. Since he obeyed the commands of these demons, David considered himself to be the Son of Sam.

**33** The Son of Sam wasn't the only serial killer to attack young women in the 1970s. Theodore "Ted" Bundy went on a killing spree from 1973 to 1978 and eventually confessed to over twenty-eight murders. He received the sentence of death not once but three times. But was he ever executed?

## 33

**ANSWER**

**Yes.** After receiving the death sentence three times (for the murders of Kimberly Leach, Lisa Levy, and Margaret Bowman) and after numerous appeals and delays, Ted Bundy was finally executed in Florida on January 24, 1989.

**34** Which serial killer has the notorious distinction of being convicted of more murders than anyone else in American history?

**(a)** Richard Ramirez

**(b)** The Boston Strangler

**(c)** John Wayne Gacy

**(d)** Charles Manson

## 34

**ANSWER**

**(c).** John Wayne Gacy, who murdered thirty-three young men in the 1970s, has the distinction of being convicted of the most murders in American history. Even more disturbingly, the bodies of the majority of these young men were buried underneath the house where he lived.

**35** Jeffrey Dahmer was another serial killer who shocked the nation. Heads, skulls, and other bodily parts of his victims were found in his apartment in Milwaukee, Wisconsin, in 1991. He kept gruesome photographs of each step of the killings. He even admitted to eating the flesh of several of the men he killed. But is it true or false that two of his victims were brothers?

## 35

**ANSWER**

Shockingly enough, the answer is **true**. In 1988, Jeffrey Dahmer was convicted of sexual exploitation of a child and second-degree assault. While that child survived, his older brother was later killed by Dahmer in 1991.

**36** Charles Manson is probably the best-known criminal mind in American history. Photographs of him are absolutely chilling, and his very name has practically become synonymous with evil. But did Charles Manson ever kill anyone with his own hands?

## 36

**ANSWER**

As far as we know, the answer is **no**. Although Manson and four of his followers were found guilty of murder in the first degree and conspiracy to commit murder in the Tate-LaBianca case, there has never been any proof that Manson killed anyone with his own hands. Charles Manson, by the way, was later found guilty of having ordered the murders of Gary Hinman and Donald Shea.

**Ugh. Enough with the serial killers. Let's lighten the mood a little with some heroes. The next few questions will test your knowledge of African-American heroes throughout our country's history:**

**37** One of the great heroines of American history is Harriet Tubman, one of the most famous "conductors" of the Underground Railroad. Her name has become inextricably linked with the elaborate system of hiding places and "safe houses" that escaped slaves were able to rely on as they made their way north. Very few people know, however, that Harriet Tubman never actually traveled the Underground Railroad herself. Is this statement true or false?

### ANSWER

**False.** Harriet Tubman made at least nineteen trips along the Underground Railroad and is credited with freeing over 300 slaves.

**38** One of the most prominent African-American leaders in the late 1800s opened the Tuskegee Institute, which taught practical skills to African-Americans in order that they might work hard, make money, and eventually buy property. He advised two presidents—Theodore Roosevelt and William Howard Taft—on racial problems and policies and also influenced the appointment of several Blacks to federal office, especially during Roosevelt's administration. What was the name of this inspiring leader?

**(a)** Booker T. Washington

**(b)** George Washington Carver

**(c)** W. E. B. Du Bois

**(d)** Sojourner Truth

## 38

**ANSWER**

**(a).** Booker T. Washington was probably the most influential African-American leader of the late nineteenth century. Though his influence started to decline in the early twentieth century thanks to a newer crop of thinkers like W. E. B. Du Bois, his remarkable journey from slave to prominent leader makes him a truly heroic figure.

**39** Of all the African-American leaders, probably none is as famous as Martin Luther King Jr. His nonviolent approach to securing civil rights for African-Americans was encapsulated in his famous and oft-quoted "I Have a Dream" speech. Where was that famous speech delivered?

**(a)** Montgomery, Alabama

**(b)** Chicago, Illinois

**(c)** Memphis, Tennessee

**(d)** Washington, D.C.

## 39

**ANSWER**

**(d).** The "I Have a Dream" speech was delivered on the steps of the Lincoln Memorial in Washington, D.C., on August 28, 1963. King was in Washington as part of the March on Washington, which was organized to bring attention to African-American unemployment and to urge Congress to pass Kennedy's civil rights bill.

**Heroes and villains sometimes have no basis in fact because, well... they're legends. In the next category, you'll decide whether these people are REAL or FICTIONAL.**

**40** First up: What about the legendary Wild West villain called Black Bart? Was he a real person or a fictional character?

### 40

**ANSWER**

The answer is a **real** person. Black Bart was a stagecoach bandit whose real name was Charles Boles. And sometimes he left a short poem for his victims.

**41** Next, most schoolkids would know the name Johnny Appleseed—but was Johnny a real person or a fictional character?

## 41

### ANSWER

The answer is a **real** person. John Chapman earned the nickname Johnny Appleseed by planting apple-tree seedlings throughout the Ohio River valley in the early nineteenth century.

**42** Stories have been handed down for generations about Texas cowboy hero Pecos Bill. But are the stories true? Was Pecos Bill real or fictional?

**42**

**ANSWER**

Pecos Bill was a **fictional** character. Real guys don't usually ride mountain lions or use rattlesnakes as a lasso. Bill did all that and lots more—before lunch.

**43** And finally, that famous symbol of the United States, your old Uncle Sam: Is he based on a real person or is Uncle Sam a fictional character?

### 43

**ANSWER**

The answer is a **real** person. In 1961 Congress passed a resolution recognizing Samuel Wilson, a New York businessman who supplied the army with meat during the War of 1812, as the real-life character who was the inspiration for and namesake of Uncle Sam.

**It's not easy to become a hero. But it's even harder to stay a hero. Let's check out some folks who got famous doing good deeds and then became infamous when they screwed up and went from hero to zero. We call this category "Fall from Grace."**

**44** Benedict Arnold: His very name is synonymous with treachery and betrayal. Yet before he became our nation's most famous traitor, Benedict Arnold was actually a hero of the Revolutionary War! He and Ethan Allen led a daring assault on Fort Ticonderoga and Arnold commanded American troops at Saratoga who bravely repulsed a British attack from Canada. But then he fell from grace. In exchange for cash, Arnold offered to surrender the fort he commanded at West Point to the British. The question is: What happened to Benedict Arnold?

**(a)** He was hanged for treason

**(b)** He escaped to England

**(c)** He was killed in battle

**(d)** He was pardoned by Washington

## 44

**ANSWER**

The answer is **(b)**. Arnold escaped to England in 1781, but by that time his treasonous behavior had disgusted the British too. Ostracized, he died a sick old man in 1801.

**45** In 1957 Charles Van Doren was America's intellectual hero. Fifty million viewers cheered for this well-bred professor when he won $129,000 on a TV quiz show. Van Doren was on the cover of *TIME* magazine; people called him "TV's... antidote to Elvis." Fan letters poured in by the thousands. Then the truth was revealed—and Van Doren fell from grace. He had seen the answers before the questions were asked! He was a FRAUD! On what popular quiz show did Van Doren appear?

**(a)** *Twenty-One*

**(b)** *The $64,000 Question*

**(c)** *The $64,000 Pyramid*

**(d)** *Break the Bank*

## 45

**ANSWER**

The answer is **(a)** *Twenty-One*. Amazingly, rigging a game show was perfectly legal at the time! The crime of Van Doren and others caught in the quiz show scandal was perjury—they lied to a grand jury about what they had done. As a result of the *Twenty-One* scandal, Congress outlawed the rigging of game shows.

**46** You can look it up in the record books: Pete Rose had more hits than any major-league baseball player in history—4,256 hits over 24 seasons. In his brilliant career Rose became one of the greatest baseball heroes of all time—only to fall far from grace. He was banned for life from major-league baseball and reduced to selling autographs on a home-shopping channel. The reason: Pete Rose gambled on sports. But here's the big question: Has Pete Rose ever admitted to betting on baseball games?

**(a)** Yes

**(b)** No

**(c)** Well, sort of

### 46

**ANSWER**

The answer is **(b)**: Pete Rose has never admitted it. And when former president Jimmy Carter investigated the Rose case, he concluded that "evidence about specifically betting on baseball is less than compelling." One thing seems certain: Fans will debate this one forever.

**And now for some questions about one of America's most revered musical heroes: Elvis Presley.**

**47** Known as the King of Rock and Roll, Elvis Presley is certainly one of the heroes of American music. But this good ole Southern boy didn't shirk his duties as an American citizen either. Elvis Aron Presley joined the U.S. Army on March 24, 1958, left active duty on March 5, 1960, and received his discharge from the Army Reserve on March 23, 1964. Where was "The King" stationed overseas during his years of active service?

- **(a)** Germany
- **(b)** France
- **(c)** Vietnam
- **(d)** Korea

## 47

### ANSWER

**(a)**. Presley served in Germany from October 1, 1958, until March 2, 1960, as a member of the 1st Medium Tank Battalion, 32nd Armor. For the first five days of that period he belonged to Company D of the battalion, and thereafter to the battalion's headquarters company at Friedberg.

**48** Elvis became notorious for those swiveling hips of his as soon as he made his debut on American television. On what television show did Elvis make his debut?

**(a)** *The Milton Berle Show*

**(b)** *The Ed Sullivan Show*

**(c)** *Stage Show*

**(d)** *The Steve Allen Show*

## 48

**ANSWER**

**(c)**. Though Elvis's appearances on *The Ed Sullivan Show* were probably his most well known, Elvis's first television appearance was on *Stage Show* on January 28, 1956.

**49** In 1973 Elvis received a gift engraved: "You Are the Greatest." What was it?

**(a)** A pair of cufflinks from Richard Nixon

**(b)** A guitar from John Lennon

**(c)** Boxing gloves from Muhammad Ali

**(d)** A diamond bracelet from Sammy Davis Jr.

### 49

**ANSWER**

**(c)**. The boxing gloves he received from Muhammad Ali proved to be among Elvis's most prized possessions.

**For decades, America's representatives of evil incarnate were the Reds, the Commies, the people in Russia who might someday bomb our cities or subvert our all-American way of life. But some feel this man was even more terrifying than the Communist threat. His name was Joseph McCarthy.**

**50** For Senator Joseph McCarthy, it all started in Wheeling, West Virginia, in 1950. He spiced up a mundane speech by claiming to hold, in his own hands, the names of 205 Communists in the U.S. State Department. But when asked by reporters that day, McCarthy would not produce the names on his list. Why was that?

**(a)** He lied about having a list

**(b)** The list was an FBI secret

**(c)** McCarthy's close friend was on the list

**(d)** McCarthy himself was on the list

HEROES AND VILLAINS

## 50

**ANSWER**

The answer is **(a)**. Following his outrageous claim, a Senate committee led by Millard Tydings challenged McCarthy to prove his statement about the so-called list. For a period of two months, McCarthy and his team grilled numerous people in a hunt for Communists, but they were unable to find a single one.

**51** As McCarthy unfairly accused hundreds of innocent U.S. citizens of Communist affiliations, he was branded a fraud by the Tydings Committee in the Senate. But McCarthy's supporters were vindictive people: What did they do to attack Senator Tydings?

**(a)** Wiretapped his home and offices

**(b)** Doctored a photo to show Tydings with a Communist

**(c)** Planted drugs in Tydings's office

**(d)** Implied that Tydings was having an extramarital affair

## 51

**ANSWER**

The answer is **(b)**. McCarthy's supporters produced a photograph in which Senator Tydings was having an intimate conversation with Communist party leader Earl Browder—but the conversation never happened! Although McCarthy claimed he had nothing to do with this, his supporters used the doctored-photo trick again to intimidate the U.S. Army!

**52** From 1950 until early 1954, McCarthy's ruthless accusations went mostly unchecked. McCarthy was out of control, accusing everyone up to and including President Eisenhower of Cold War evils. But in 1954 McCarthy's reign of terror imploded with his attack on the army. What all-American institution helped lead to the Senator's downfall?

**(a)** The Supreme Court

**(b)** The American Civil Liberties Union

**(c)** Television

**(d)** The Post Office

## 52

**ANSWER**

The answer is **(c)**. In March 1954, Edward R. Murrow exposed McCarthy in three episodes of *See It Now!*, his television news magazine. Then things got worse. McCarthy's attacks on the army were televised live for thirty-six days—and viewers were stunned by the senator's illogical arguments, aggressive tactics, and generally despicable behavior. Less than a year later, the Senate censured Joe McCarthy. And in 1957 the hard-drinking senator died from cirrhosis of the liver. He was forty-seven years old.

**53** Although McCarthy's "Red Scare" is probably the most well known, the Red Scare that occurred thirty years earlier stirred up the country just as much. With Communism just taking hold in Russia, Americans in 1919 were afraid of anything remotely communistic or socialistic—in fact, they began to be afraid of anything foreign. As a result of this hysteria, the popularity of the Ku Klux Klan soared, Sacco and Vanzetti were unfairly tried and summarily executed, and mass arrests and deportations became much more common. Who was the man responsible for the Red Scare of 1919?

**(a)** J. Edgar Hoover

**(b)** J. C. Walter

**(c)** Mitchell Palmer

**(d)** Woodrow Wilson

## ANSWER

**(c)**. A. Mitchell Palmer, President Wilson's attorney general, is generally credited with causing the Red Scare of 1919. After a bomb exploded outside his house, Palmer went on a rampage to purge the United States of any suspected Communists, socialists, or anarchists.

**54** Another corrupted politician in American history was William Marcy Tweed, the "Boss" of New York's Tammany Hall. During the mid-1800s, Boss Tweed made tens of millions of dollars by manipulating votes, bribing politicians, giving and taking kickbacks—you name it, Boss Tweed did it. What position in New York City's government did Boss Tweed hold that enabled him to exert such control?

**(a)** Mayor

**(b)** Manhattan borough president

**(c)** Chief of the Department of Public Works

**(d)** New York City comptroller

## 54

**ANSWER**

**(c)**. Although William Marcy Tweed was technically only the chief of the Department of Public Works, his status as the head of Tammany Hall, one of the many fraternal organizations that had its roots in the post-Revolution era, really gave him the power he wielded. Tweed was arrested in 1872 and died in prison after giving a full confession to all of the crimes he committed while in office.

**Hillary Rodham Clinton once said "It takes a villain to raise a hero." Or something that sounded almost like that. Sometimes it's tough to tell the heroes from the villains without a scorecard. We call this category "You Decide."**

**55** To many, he was J. Edgar Hoover—HERO. He was the man who made the FBI one of the world's top police organizations. As FBI chief, he demanded that agents meet rigorous standards. He promoted scientific methods like fingerprinting and established a "most wanted" list to capture the worst criminals. But to others, he was J. Edgar Hoover—VILLAIN. He was a man who abused his powers. Under Hoover, the FBI investigated, wiretapped, and intimidated anyone he perceived as a threat: Martin Luther King. John Lennon. Homosexuals. Even presidents in office! And Hoover did it for a very long time. He was named head of the FBI in 1924—how long did he stay in power?

**(a)** 10 years   **(c)** 48 years

**(b)** 38 years  **(d)** 58 years

## 55

**ANSWER**

The answer is **(c)**. Only his death in 1972 could separate Hoover from the FBI. But with that question answered, one remains: Was J. Edgar Hoover a hero or a villain? You decide!

**56** Is he an angel of mercy or Dr. Death? Opinions couldn't be more divided over Jack Kevorkian, who made headlines when he began to help incurably ill patients commit suicide. He even built a "suicide machine" that delivers a lethal dose of drugs with the flip of a switch. Over the years, Dr. Kevorkian has helped some 130 people to die. But where and when did he perform his first assisted suicide?

**(a)** Illinois in 1984

**(b)** Wisconsin in 1988

**(c)** Michigan in 1990

**(d)** Las Vegas in 1992

## 56

**ANSWER**

The answer is **(c)**. Dr. Kevorkian's final words to his first suicide patient were "Have a nice trip." If nothing else, Jack Kevorkian forced the right-to-die debate into the national spotlight. But is he a villain who violated the Hippocratic oath, or a hero who eased the pain of those most in need? You decide!

Here are a few more questions about supervillains. This time they're from television. We'll give you the name of the villain, you name the hero.

**57** The dirty deeds of villain Oil Can Harry were often interrupted by the hero's cry: "Here I come to save the day!" Name the super rodent who sang that song.

**ANSWER**

That cry could only mean that 1950s TV hero **Mighty Mouse** was on his way.

**58** Natasha Fatale was a well-known villain, but you probably never knew her last name. Who were the heroes?

**58**

**ANSWER**

The heroes were **Rocky and Bullwinkle**. And you'd recognize Ms. Fatale instantly if she was standing next to her fellow no-good-nik, Boris Badenov.

**59** Some villains are organized. Take, for example, the evil superspies at THRUSH. What organization did they battle in the mid-1960s on NBC?

**ANSWER**

The United Network Command for Law and Enforcement, otherwise known as **UNCLE**. Give yourself extra credit if you remember the men from UNCLE: Napoleon Solo and Ilya Kuryakin.

**60** And finally, the villains were Egghead, Mr. Freeze, and King Tut. Who was the good guy?

**60**

**ANSWER**

The answer, of course, is **Batman**, who was played by Adam West in the 1960s television series.

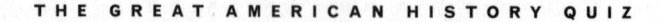

**61** Actually, the actions of this next hero paved the way for the Batmobile: Henry Ford emerged as one of the heroes of the 1920s. Born into a poor immigrant family, he rose to become one of the great pioneers of the automotive industry. Thanks to the assembly line, and to the relatively generous wages he paid his employees, the Model-T Ford was one of the first automobiles that was affordable to the working classes—and as a result, the automotive industry became one of the cornerstones of the American economy. Which of the following innovations did Henry Ford actually invent?

**(a)** The automobile

**(b)** The assembly line

**ANSWER**

The answer, surprisingly enough, is **neither**. Although you could argue that Henry Ford is responsible for popularizing both the automobile and the assembly line, neither of these ideas were his own. The assembly line was an idea dreamed up by Frederick Taylor, and the invention of the automobile can be credited to a number of different people—Gottlieb Daimler, Wilhelm Maybach, and Karl Benz—but not to Ford.

**For most of this century, the word "hero" represented a pretty simple concept. A hero was a guy who caught bad guys. Or a hunk of Italian bread stuffed with fatty meats. Or someone who played baseball for a team like the New York Yankees ...**

**62** Lou Gehrig was a quiet man who did his job without fanfare. He played 2,130 games in a row—that's fourteen years without missing a game. Plus he hit over .300 for twelve straight seasons and still holds the record for most career grand slams. For all of this, as well as his sportsmanship and courage, Gehrig may have been the Yankees' greatest all-time hero. And he earned a hero's nickname too. What was it?

  **(a)** Old Reliable

  **(b)** The Iron Horse

  **(c)** The Yankee Clipper

  **(d)** The Louisville Slugger

## 62

**ANSWER**

The answer is **(b)**. But during the 1939 season the Iron Horse finally faltered. He was diagnosed with ALS, now known as Lou Gehrig's disease. Two years later, Gehrig was dead, leaving behind a hero's legacy.

**63** Shortly before he died, Mickey Mantle summed up his drinking problems and other demons by saying "God gave me everything and I blew it. For the kids out there, don't be like me!" But for many of us growing up in the 1950s and '60s, Mickey Mantle was the ultimate hero, accomplishing the ultimate heroic task: hitting home runs. So much about baseball—and heroes—has changed forever. But three of Mantle's records remain. Which of the following is one of them:

**(a)** Most inside-the-park home runs

**(b)** Most back-to-back home runs

**(c)** Most 500-foot home runs

**(d)** Most World Series home runs

## 63

**ANSWER**

The answer is **(d)**. In a dozen World Series appearances, Mantle hit a total of eighteen home runs. He also holds Series records for most runs and most RBIs. As Bob Costas eulogized, "For reasons that no statistics, no dry recitation of facts can possibly capture, he was the most compelling baseball hero of our lifetime."

**64** In his final at-bat of the 1972 season, Roberto Clemente joined baseball's immortals by notching his 3000th hit. No one knew then it would be his last. You see, Clemente was the pride of Latinos, a native son who often went home to Puerto Rico, where he taught kids and raised money to help people. So when an earthquake struck Latin America in December of 1972, Clemente decided to personally rush needed supplies to the victims. But his cargo plane exploded just minutes after takeoff. Where was Roberto Clemente going when he died?

**(a)** Nicaragua

**(b)** Cuba

**(c)** Puerto Rico

**(d)** Venezuela

## 64

**ANSWER**

The answer is **(a)**. Clemente, the first Latino elected into baseball's Hall of Fame, once said, "If you have the opportunity to make things better and you don't, then you are wasting your time on this earth."

What does your typical "hero" do? You probably visualize some musclebound guy, chest out, feet firmly planted on some enormous cliff, music blaring, with an American flag unfurled in the background. And what does our ideal heroine look like? Well, first off, she's probably got more sense. Let's look at some American heroines.

**65** This female tennis player landed what the *London Times* called "the drop shot and volley heard around the world" when she defeated self-proclaimed "male chauvinist pig" and former Wimbledon winner Bobby Riggs in a 1973 "Battle of the Sexes" tennis match. Although this was probably her most famous victory, her career achievements include six Wimbledon singles championships and four U.S. Open titles. She was also ranked No. 1 in the world five years. Who is this?

**(a)** Margaret Court

**(b)** Martina Navratilova

**(c)** Chris Evert

**(d)** Billie Jean King

### 65

**ANSWER**

**(d)**. In addition to being one of the greatest tennis players the world has ever known, Billie Jean King is a tireless promoter of women's sports and for gender equity in all athletic competitions.

**66** Think you're busy? Listen to this résumé:

1852: Founded New Jersey's first free school

Early 1860s: Delivered supplies to the front lines during the Civil War

1865: Organized the Bureau of Records and helped find some 20,000 Civil War MIAs

1882: Lobbied the United States to ratify the Geneva Convention, setting rules for humane conduct during war

1889: Led relief effort for Johnstown Flood victims

Which remarkable woman gets credit for all these achievements?

**(a)** Florence Nightingale

**(b)** Jane Addams

**(c)** Susan B. Anthony

**(d)** Clara Barton

### ANSWER

The answer is **(d)** Clara Barton, who is probably best known for one accomplishment we left off her résumé—which leads us to our next question.

**67** True or false: Clara Barton, known as the "Angel of the Battlefield" during the Civil War for her tireless efforts to take care of wounded soldiers, founded the International Red Cross.

## 67

**ANSWER**

**False**: Clara Barton founded the *American Red Cross* in 1821 and served as its president until she retired at the ripe young age of eighty-two. The irony of the situation is that she was not even allowed to officially work for the International Red Cross during the Franco-Prussian War because she was a woman. She did, however, volunteer to serve as an independent relief worker in Strasbourg, France, from 1870 to 1871.

**68** Helen Keller was one of the most remarkable women in American history. Despite being deaf and blind, she grew up to become a world-famous author and social activist. Keller was completely mute until she was taught to communicate by an extraordinary teacher named Anne Sullivan. And surprisingly, it was another famous American who helped bring Helen and Anne together. Who was it?

**(a)** Thomas Edison

**(b)** William Jennings Bryan

**(c)** Alexander Graham Bell

**(d)** Grover Cleveland

**HEROES AND VILLAINS**

## 68

**ANSWER**

The answer is **(c)**: It was Alexander Graham Bell who advised Helen's parents to get her a teacher. And with Anne Sullivan's guidance, Keller learned to communicate and truly flourished. In an age when few women even went to college, Keller graduated with honors from Radcliffe in 1904. She went on to write numerous books and became the world's leading advocate for the deaf and blind.

**69** Another question about this truly great American heroine—True or false: Helen Keller was born blind and deaf.

## 69

### ANSWER

**False**. Helen Keller was born a healthy child on June 27, 1880, in Tuscumbia, Alabama. In 1882 Helen was left deaf, blind, and mute by an illness diagnosed as brain fever that may have been scarlet fever.

**70** Charles Lindbergh wasn't the only American pilot to quite literally soar to great heights of fame. American women and men alike cheered for the success of Amelia Earhart, who became an overnight sensation when she flew across the Atlantic in 1928. Nine years later she attempted to fly around the world, but her plane went down somewhere over the Pacific Ocean. Neither her plane nor her body were ever recovered. But we're not going to ask you what happened to her plane. We do, however, want to know if the following statement is true or false: When Amelia Earhart's plane went down, she was the only one in it.

## 70

**ANSWER**

**False.** Amelia wasn't planning to fly the plane around the world alone. Her navigator, a man by the name of Fred Noonan, was also in the plane when it mysteriously disappeared.

**71** Segregation ruled Montgomery, Alabama, and Rosa Parks, for one, was tired of it. She despised the Blacks-only elevators and usually walked up the stairs instead. For similar reasons, she rarely took buses. Instead of riding like a second-class citizen, she walked. But on December 1, 1955, Parks was tired and took the bus. And when a White man demanded that she give up her seat, Parks refused. Where was she sitting at the time?

**(a)** In the front of the bus

**(b)** In the back of the bus

**(c)** In the middle of the bus

## 71

**ANSWER**

The answer is **(c)** in the middle of the bus. On Montgomery city buses, the front rows were for Whites, while the middle and back rows were for Blacks. But Whites could *demand* the middle seats when needed. And if one White passenger wanted to sit down, Blacks had to clear the whole row of seats. On that day in 1955, Rosa Parks refused to move and was arrested. In response, Martin Luther King led a bus boycott that lasted more than a year, until the Supreme Court ruled against Montgomery's segregation laws. It was a defining moment in the civil rights movement.

**72** Although most people are familiar with Rosa Parks and her refusal to give up her seat on the bus, fewer people would probably be familiar with the woman who, almost fifty years before, refused to give up her seat on a train to go into the smoking car, which was reserved for African-Americans. She successfully sued the railroad for making her give up her seat. Though that decision was soon overruled by the state court, this civil rights–minded woman went on to become part owner of a newspaper and was particularly outspoken against the lynching of Blacks in the South. She was also one of the founders of the NAACP. Who was this accomplished heroine?

**(a)** Mary McLeod Bethune

**(b)** Mary Ann Shadd Cary

**(c)** Madame C. J. Walker

**(d)** Ida B. Wells-Barnett

## 72

### ANSWER

**(d)**. Though all of the African-American women above are heroines in their own right, the correct answer to this question is Ida B. Wells-Barnett.

**73** When her thirteen-year-old daughter, Cari, was killed by a drunken driver in 1980, this American heroine joined together with other mothers in California and formed Mothers Against Drunk Driving (MADD). MADD currently has over 600 chapters throughout the United States and is one of the loudest voices condemning drinking and driving. Who was the founder of this impressive organization?

**(a)** Candy Lightner

**(b)** Jennifer Harbury

**(c)** Julia Quinlan

**(d)** Rebecca Pruslin

## 73

**ANSWER**

**(a).** When Candy Lightner discovered that the man who killed her daughter while driving under the influence of alcohol had been accused of three other drunk-driving incidents, she quit her job as a real estate agent and organized the first chapter of MADD.

**74** It was one small step for Sally Ride and one giant leap for women everywhere when Ride became the first American woman in space in 1983. What was the name of the space shuttle on which she took her historic ride into history?

**(a)** *Voyager*

**(b)** *Challenger*

**(c)** *Apollo*

**(d)** *Discovery*

### 74

**ANSWER**

**(b)**. Sally Ride became the first American woman in space when she climbed on board the *Challenger* on June 18, 1983. She was a mission specialist whose duties included assisting the commander and the pilot on ascent, reentry, and landing. She boarded the *Challenger* again in 1984 on a second mission.

**75** In 1897 Alice McLellan Birney and Phoebe Apperson Hearst established this national organization devoted to child welfare and were elected its first president and vice president. What is the name of the organization they established?

  (a) PTA

  (b) UNICEF

  (c) United Way

  (d) Catholic Charities

## 75

**ANSWER**

**(a)**. Get out your baking tins and get ready for a cake sale! Alice McLellan Birney and Phoebe Apperson Hearst founded the PTA at the end of the nineteenth century. Today the national PTA has nearly 6.5 million members working in 26,000 local chapters in all fifty states, the District of Columbia, the U.S. Virgin Islands, and in Department of Defense schools in the Pacific and Europe.

**76** The first Black woman to win the Pulitzer prize was an American poet and children's-book author who grew up on the gritty south side of Chicago. *Annie Allen,* a series of poems following the life of a Black girl from childhood to adulthood, took the literary world by storm when it won the Pulitzer in 1950. What is the name of this prominent poet?

**(a)** Gwendolyn Brooks

**(b)** Maya Angelou

**(c)** Alice Walker

**(d)** Toni Morrison

**76**

**ANSWER**

**(a).** Gwendolyn Brooks became the first African-American woman to win the Pulitzer prize.

**77** The first woman to found a lasting, American-based religion, this notable heroine was also a successful journalist and author: Her book *Science and Health* went on to sell over eight million copies. What is the name of this remarkable nineteenth-century woman?

**(a)** Dorothea Dix

**(b)** Ellen White

**(c)** Mary Baker Eddy

**(d)** Lucretia Mott

## 77

### ANSWER

**(c).** Mary Baker Eddy founded the First Church of Christ, Scientist (commonly called Christian Scientists), in 1879. In addition to establishing this thriving religion, she also founded a publishing company, obtained a charter for the Massachusetts Metaphysical College as a degree-granting institution, and founded the *Christian Science Journal* (later the *Christian Science Sentinel*) and the *Christian Science Monitor.* Not bad for a home-schooled woman from New Hampshire!

**78** And although the Roman Catholic Church may have been around a bit longer than the church Mary Baker Eddy founded, it wasn't until 1946 that the first American saint was canonized—and she was a woman to boot! Who was the first American to be made a Catholic saint?

**(a)** Elizabeth Ann Seton

**(b)** Dorothy Day

**(c)** Mother Jones

**(d)** Frances Xavier Cabrini

## 78

**ANSWER**

**(d)**. Although Elizabeth Seton was the first American-born woman to be canonized a saint in the Roman Catholic Church, Frances Xavier Cabrini became the first American saint when she was canonized in 1946. Though born in Italy, Frances Xavier Cabrini became a citizen in 1909. Appropriately enough, she is now the patron saint of immigrants!

**79** Not content to be merely a part of one of America's most powerful political families, this noble woman distinguished herself in her own right by founding the Special Olympics. From its humble beginnings, the Special Olympics has grown tremendously: Nearly one million athletes in 130 countries now compete worldwide in twenty-two sports. More than 15,000 games, meets, and tournaments are held annually. Who established this most remarkable organization?

**(a)** Lady Bird Johnson

**(b)** Eleanor Roosevelt

**(c)** Eunice Kennedy Shriver

**(d)** Mamie Eisenhower

## 79

**ANSWER**

**(c).** In 1984 Ronald Reagan awarded Eunice Kennedy Shriver the Presidential Medal of Freedom for her unceasing work on behalf of the mentally handicapped.

**80** The Citadel in South Carolina is one of this country's oldest and most respected military colleges, and it has produced a number of American heroes. But one of its most courageous heroes is actually a heroine. On January 20, 1994, this notable heroine became the first woman to enroll in the previously all-male institution, paving the way for other women to enter the prestigious college. What was the name of the first woman to enroll in the Citadel?

**(a)** Jeanie Mentavlos

**(b)** Kim Messer

**(c)** Shannon Faulkner

**(d)** Maryanne Stropoli

# 80

**ANSWER**

**(c).** Shannon Faulkner was the first woman to enroll as a freshman in the Citadel—but . . .

**81** Is the following statement true or false: She was also the first woman to graduate from the Citadel.

## 81

**ANSWER**

**False**. After months of legal battles, Shannon Faulkner left the Citadel six days into "Hell Week," the school's infamous orientation for new students. The first woman to graduate from the Citadel was Nancy Mace, who received her diploma in 1999.

**Daniel Boone and Davy Crockett were two of our most celebrated wilderness heroes and fashion pioneers. But which was which? The answer to each of the following questions is either "Boone" or "Crockett."**

**82** During this fad from the 1950s, kids across America wore coonskin caps, just like him: Boone or Crockett?

**82**

**ANSWER**

The answer is **Davy Crockett**, the "King of the Wild Frontier."

**83** Who called his Kentucky rifle Old Tick-Licker, because it could shoot a tick off the rump of an animal? Was it Boone or Crockett?

**83**

ANSWER

**Daniel Boone.**

**84** Who became a Tennessee congressman—and argued constantly with President Andrew Jackson?

## 84

### ANSWER

The answer is Congressman **Davy Crockett**.

**85** Who fought at the Alamo, where he died at the age of forty-nine, in 1836? Was the hero Boone or Crockett?

**85**

**ANSWER**

Once again the answer is **Crockett**. Daniel Boone lived to the ripe old age of eighty-five.

**86** Speaking of the Alamo, who can't be impressed by the heroic courage shown by the three thousand men who sacrificed their lives in this famous battle in American history? Unfortunately, all but three of the three thousand Americans at the Alamo perished—including the general who so bravely led his men in the battle. Who was in command of the American forces at the Alamo?

**(a)** Stephen F. Austin

**(b)** General Santa Anna

**(c)** William B. Travis

**(d)** Sam Houston

## 86

**ANSWER**

**(c)**. Colonel William B. Travis was in command of the Alamo during that fateful battle in 1836.

**87** Wild Bill Hickock is another true cowboy of the American West. He was a frontier scout, peace officer, stagecoach driver, a marshal, a sheriff, and a gambler. In fact, it was while gambling in 1876 that he met his end. Rumor has it that he was shot dead by a Mr. Jack McCall in the Number 10 Saloon—while holding a combination of cards that is now known as "the dead man's hand." What is "the dead man's hand"?

### 87

**ANSWER**

A pair of black aces and a pair of black eights.

**Every day, heroes and villains face off in our court system, and never are the roles of hero and villain more defined than in those unique battles that we call "trials of the century." Of course, as we saw in the O.J. trial, the villain to some is a hero to others. As it turns out, that's not so unusual in a trial of the century.**

**88** The 1954 murder trial of Dr. Sam Sheppard was so sensational, it inspired the hit TV series and movie *The Fugitive*. Like the character Dr. Richard Kimble, Sheppard said he was wrongly accused of murdering his wife and that a mysterious intruder was the real killer. But with the evidence and publicity heavily against him, Sheppard was found guilty and sentenced to life. The question is: Whatever happened to Dr. Sam Sheppard?

**(a)** He escaped and found the intruder

**(b)** He died in prison

**(c)** He is still in prison

**(d)** DNA evidence supported his innocence

HEROES AND VILLAINS

## 88

**ANSWER**

The answer is **(d)**. After serving ten years, Sheppard won a new trial and was later acquitted. But questions of his guilt still lingered. So after Sheppard died in 1970, his son vowed to clear his name. Finally, in 1998, DNA tests revealed that blood found at the crime scene didn't belong to either Sheppard or his wife—was it the mysterious intruder's?

**89** In the New Jersey courtroom was Charles Lindbergh—one of the world's greatest living heroes—facing Bruno Hauptmann, the alleged villain accused of kidnapping and murdering Lindbergh's infant son. As you know, Hauptmann was found guilty and later executed. Is the following statement true or false: After being sentenced to death, Hauptmann could have saved his own life by confessing to the crime.

### 89

**ANSWER**

The answer is **true**. Hauptmann was offered a deal: life in prison in exchange for a confession. But he chose death by maintaining his innocence. Though the evidence against him seemed strong, there were many lingering doubts—even New Jersey's governor tried to have the case reopened. So . . . was the wrong man cast as the villain and then executed in this trial of the century?

**90** The scene was a Tennessee courtroom purgatory, where temperatures topped a hundred degrees and emotions ran much hotter. In a way, the famous Scopes monkey trial forced a jury to decide between God and science. William Jennings Bryan represented the State of Tennessee, whose legislature had passed a law banning the teaching of any doctrine that opposed the divine creation of man. The eloquent Clarence Darrow represented John Scopes, a high-school science teacher. At issue was the book Scopes used to teach evolution. What was that book?

**(a)** Darwin's *Origin of Species*

**(b)** *Planet of the Apes*

**(c)** A standard biology textbook

**(d)** *The Descent of Man*

## 90

**ANSWER**

The answer is **(c)**. Scopes used *Hunter's Civic Biology*—but so did all science teachers at his school! So why was Scopes in court? It was all a setup: The ACLU wanted to test the legality of Tennessee's law, so they convinced Scopes to stand trial, then built a media circus around him. Scopes was found guilty but was fined only a hundred dollars. And Tennessee's law stayed on the books until 1967.

**It's time now for a regular category on The Great American History Quiz: "Who Said It?" See if you can identify the speakers of the following quotes:**

**91** Let's start with a good guy. Referring to himself, he said: "It's just a job. Grass grows, birds fly, waves pound the sand. I beat people up." Who said that?

**(a)** Jesse Ventura

**(b)** Arnold Schwarzenegger

**(c)** Muhammad Ali

**(d)** Sugar Ray Leonard

### 91

**ANSWER**

The answer is **(c)** Muhammad Ali.

**92** Sometimes the difference between a hero and a villain depends upon your point of view. Who once said: "Show me a hero and I will write you a tragedy"?

**(a)** F. Scott Fitzgerald

**(b)** Teddy Roosevelt

**(c)** Orson Welles

**(d)** Ernest Hemingway

## 92

**ANSWER**

The answer is **(a)**. F. Scott Fitzgerald could easily have been describing his own life story.

**93** And which deep thinker came up with this idea: "To my mind, to kill in war is not a whit better than to commit an ordinary murder"?

**(a)** Charles Manson

**(b)** Martin Luther King Jr.

**(c)** Bob Dylan

**(d)** Albert Einstein

## 93

### ANSWER

The answer is **(d)** Albert Einstein, who was always conflicted about his contributions to the development of the atomic bomb.

**Sometimes heroes are ordinary people. In the course of their daily lives, something extraordinary happens. And for a brief shining moment, the nation watches.**

**94** On October 16, 1987, the world held its breath as a heroic team of volunteers finally reached eighteen-month-old Jessica McClure. "Baby Jessica" had fallen down a well pipe just eight inches wide in her aunt's backyard. Millions watched the valiant rescue attempt, live on television. Do you remember how long Baby Jessica was trapped in the well?

**(a)** A week

**(b)** Two and a half days

**(c)** One day

**(d)** Fifteen hours

## 94

**ANSWER**

The answer is **(b)**. For fifty-eight hours, almost a hundred rescuers worked around the clock, using diamond-tipped drills to cut a twenty-nine-foot-deep shaft through the bedrock. Finally, a paramedic carefully pulled Baby Jessica out of the narrow hole and lifted her to freedom. Sometimes it really does take a village.

**95** Mostly, Ryan White was an ordinary thirteen-year-old kid. But he was also a hemophiliac— and when Ryan was diagnosed with AIDS following a blood transfusion, his classmates and their parents became terrified. It was 1985, and people didn't know much about how AIDS was spread. Parents pulled their kids out of school, a gunshot was fired into Ryan's home, and at church people refused to shake his hand. Who did Ryan say was the first public figure to speak out in his defense?

**(a)** Elton John

**(b)** NYC mayor Ed Koch

**(c)** Tom Hanks

**(d)** Michael Jackson

## 95

**ANSWER**

The answer is **(b)** Ed Koch. Before he died, Ryan's family moved and he finally found acceptance at Hamilton Heights High School, in Cicero, Indiana, a small town near Indianapolis. To put it in Ryan's words: "I'm just one of the kids, and all because the students . . . listened to the facts, educated their parents . . . and believed in me."

**96** Secret Service agent Clint Hill was one of John F. Kennedy's favorite bodyguards. In fact, he was traveling behind JFK's car in the fateful Dallas motorcade. When shots rang out, Hill courageously jumped onto the car to shield the president and First Lady. Although decorated for his bravery, Hill had blamed himself for reacting too slowly to save the president. What 1993 film was based on Clint Hill's story?

**(a)** *JFK*

**(b)** *The Body Guard*

**(c)** *In the Line of Fire*

**(d)** *Absolute Power*

## 96

**ANSWER**

The answer is **(c)**. In the movie, the fictional character based on Hill redeems himself in a heroic Hollywood ending. But in real life, Clint Hill has been unable to shake his demons over the incident.

**Clint Hill may have been one of the few cut-and-dry heroes of the Kennedy assassination. But there are scores of people who can easily be called villains thanks to their role in JFK's murder. We'll end the book with a few questions about the oft-investigated, always controversial case.**

**97** Did Lee Harvey Oswald act alone in killing John F. Kennedy or was he part of a conspiracy? The Warren Commission determined that Oswald was solely responsible for the president's death, but rumors about his involvement in the assassination have been flying since that day in 1963. Which of these statements about Lee Harvey Oswald is *false*?

**(a)** He was held for three weeks in a youth center for skipping school.

**(b)** He was once court-martialed for shooting himself while in the Marine Corps.

**(c)** He once taught third grade.

**(d)** He was once arrested for disturbing the peace while giving out political leaflets.

## 97

**ANSWER**

All of the above are true except for **(c)**. Lee Harvey Oswald was never a schoolteacher.

**98** John F. Kennedy wasn't the only man Lee Harvey Oswald supposedly killed on November 22, 1963. Less than one hour after he allegedly assassinated the president, Lee Harvey Oswald shot and killed a police officer. What was the name of the police officer?

**(a)** Cecil McWatters

**(b)** Roger Craig

**(c)** J. D. Tippit

**(d)** James Tague

## 98

**ANSWER**

**(c)**. Officer J. D. Tippit was killed by Oswald on the same day as the assassination.

**99** With all the hoopla surrounding the Kennedy assassination, many people forget that he wasn't the only one injured by Oswald's gunshot. John Connally, who was sitting in the president's limousine, was critically wounded in the attack. But your question is this: Why was John Connally sitting with the president?

**(a)** He was driving the car

**(b)** He was the governor of Texas

**(c)** He was the mayor of Dallas

**(d)** He was the first Democratic senator of Texas ever elected

## 99

**ANSWER**

**(b).** James Connally was the governor of the state of Texas. He died in 1993, at the age of seventy-five.

**100** There are, however, those who believe that Lee Harvey Oswald wasn't a villain—that he didn't kill the president at all. There are some, for example, who believe that a man named Louis Witt may have played an important role in the assassination. Louis Witt, better known as the "Umbrella Man," was standing in Dealey Plaza with an open umbrella on the day of the murder. When tracked down by the House Select Committee on Assassinations, Mr. Witt explained that he was holding an open umbrella in an act of political protest. What was the Umbrella Man protesting?

- **(a)** The handling of the Cuban Missile Crisis
- **(b)** Joseph Kennedy Sr.'s appeasement of Hitler
- **(c)** The Bay of Pigs invasion
- **(d)** John F. Kennedy's civil rights bill

**ANSWER**

**(b)**. Louis Witt claimed that the open umbrella was to remind President Kennedy of his father's support of British Prime Minister Neville Chamberlain when the former was U.S. ambassador to England. Witt believed that both Chamberlain and Kennedy Sr. were much too soft on Hitler.

**101** Perhaps part of the reason there is so much controversy surrounding Kennedy's assassination is that Oswald never stood trial. He was shot and killed by Jack Ruby just two days after his arrest. Jack Ruby's name dominated the headlines for weeks after the murder—but, oddly enough, Jack Ruby wasn't even the killer's real name. What was it?

**(a)** Joseph Rubenstein

**(b)** John Rubinowitz

**(c)** Joseph Ruby

**(d)** Jacob Rubenstein

### 101

**ANSWER**

**(d)**. Jack Ruby's real name was Jacob Rubenstein.